Spooks

By Colin and Jacqui Hawkins
and a ghost writer

Silver Burdett Company
Morristown, New Jersey

Ghosts...
are just like
you and
me except
that....

..now you see
them......
and now
you don't .

Ghost Guises

Ghosts mostly appear as floppy white sheets. (They are said to materialize.) Other spooks take different shapes. These are some you may – or may not – see.

Regular sheet ghosts (wraiths)

Headless spook

Bodiless spook

Several ghosts together are known as a shriek of ghosts.

Terrifying ghost

Terrified ghost

A singing spook.

Headless bodiless spook often mistaken for a cloud

Wooooooo oo

Invisible friendly spook

Hello

Dem bones... Dem bones

Invisible spooks make their presence felt – by booing or blowing or smelling or making your flesh creep.

pew

Invisible unfriendly spook

Well it's not me!

A skelespook

Spook Species.

Spooks can never change. When they return from the dead to haunt the living, they come as they were in life.

Accompanied by his faithful haggis, a Scottish spook plays his ghastly pipes as he stalks the castle battlements.

Oh dear
Oh dear
'tis a terrible ting...
a terrible ting

Irish Banshee

A miserable creature with bad news to tell.

Wail Wail Whine Whine

Screech! Screech!

Howl!

Can't see yoo, Jimmy

'Ay the Boo'

The Tartan Torment

The Phantom of the Opera.

Heiaha!

Scandinavian Spooks.

all pulling together after centuries of pillage and plunder

At the Palace of Versailles, Marie Antoinette endlessly offers her crumbling cake to not so poor tourists.

Aimez, vous, le gateau?

I 'ave met my Waterloo but.... 'as anyone seen Josephine?

Animal Apparitions

Even spiders
may be spooks
?

Ghastly grim and
ancient raven —
guarding ancient
treasure

Cor! Stone
the crows!
I'm not
that
bad!

A'har.
Jim l
A'har

An Old Sea Dog

Sailors do tell of wild stormy
nights when the only sound
is that of the tap tapping
of an old sea dog on the
way to his drinking bowl
in the seaport tavern.

A Famous Phantom.

The Flying Dutchman

Condemned to sail the seven seas forever, the Dutchman brings death and destruction to all who witness the passing of his ship, so DON'T LOOK AT THIS PAGE!

Dick Turpin, on his famous mare Black Bess, preys on those with full piggy banks at lonely cross walks.

The loneliest Roman of them all searches for his legion 2000 years too late.

Another Famous Phantom.

A totally unknown phantom

Quo vadis?

Your piggy or your life

or your sugar lumps

Spook horse shoes get a lot of wear.

Spook Spotting

The lights dim, a freezing draft of air whistles under
the unopened door, you hear footsteps coming towards
you, nearer, nearer, nearer, the dog whines, the door
knob turns and . . . you think you've seen a ghost?
Don't kid yourself, it's not that easy. Spooks are no fools.
You have to be really smart to spot a spook.

Most spooks are snobs, so
don't bother spook
spotting in trailer parks
or public housing projects. Go to
posh places where there
are large old houses.

Sit Sirrah.

Woof!

Typical Elizabethan mansion spook with cur.

Remember: You'll never find a spook in a trailer home.

Heads are frequently carri because of the low ceilings.

Lots of monks, nuns and priests become ghosts. So always look in churches and convents. Nuns and monks wear flapping garments for most of their lives so they are well equipped when they die. Listen for their chilling chant as they float about the cloisters a little above the cold stone floors, saying their beads.

As well as being snobbish, spooks tend to be set in their ways – they always remain at the level they knew. This only presents problems when the floor level rises rather than falls over the centuries and we witness the phenomenon of the footless ghost.

Ghostly Habits

Mother Superior. & (floats higher than the other sisters.)

A pair of holy ghosts

Straying balls are a constant nuisance.

Transports to Terror

You are walking alone along a country road. It is dark and silent, except for the rustle of horse chestnut leaves and the thud of a falling conker. Suddenly you hear the thunder of hooves, the jangle of a harness, the creaking of coach wheels. Can this be the last bus?

Cold and tired you get out the fare, but DO NOT press your silver into the conductor's icy hand. Do not be tempted. For no-one returns from a lift in the headless coachman's carriage.

There's always room in a spook's sedan chair...

For travelers who have a life time to spare...

Only another 1,000,000 years

Room for one more inside

Soon be my turn to sit down.

legs worn to the bone

Hunting the Haunting

Are you brave? Could you sit in a dark cold crypt full of scuttling spiders, with slimy things slithering across the floor and gruesome ghouls moaning and groaning and dragging their chains and creeping up behind you? If so, spook spotting is for you.

Apart from nerves and guts all you need is a pig or cat and a few essential aids.

Pen with ink - Ghosts like writing messages

Candle in holder and lots of matches *

Ball of string to find your way out of haunted houses.

* Ghosts love blowing candles out.

Egors a Sissy.

Typical Ghost message.

Spook Spotter's Guide.

Apparitions to Zombies

Successful photo of spook.

Lots of sourballs

The O'Gools

Ghosts never move. They haunt the places in which they lived. The O'Gools are typical. They try not to disrupt the nice people who now live in their house but every so often one of them slips up and gets seen. Screams, tears, terror – if only the living knew how harmless these ghosts are.

For a start there's Dad, Mr Fingal Drool O'Gool, once a teacher but now a shadow of his former self. Then there's Mommy, Ginny O'Gool, whose fondness for spirits is famous, the older children Ralph the Wraith and Mona the moaner, the identically ghastly twins, Float and Gloat, and the pets Hairy and Scary.

Mommy and Daddy teach the young ones how to haunt without hurting. But Ralph and Mona enjoy throwing on a sheet and shocking half the neighborhood. It's hard to keep them home at nights. Even the pets like to pop up in unexpected places and petrify the population.

Float   Gloat

High Fiber Diet

Ghostli pops

Gloat glas

Skimmed milk

hic!

Miaow!

At night, when the real family has gone to bed, the O'Gools materialize for breakfast. They need building up to keep fit for haunting. Like ghosts themselves, ghost food has no substance and does not comply with the law of gravity.

Nor, under the influence of the children, does the furniture. Ghosts learn to levitate when they are very young and making other objects rise into the air is the favorite game of spook children. Objects flying about a room like frisbies are usually the work of indisciplined young spooks. The O'Gools never allow their children to play such games.

Breakfast each night
keeps a ghost ghostie
white.
(Old ghost proverb.)

Work for Weirdos.

Shh!

Dog's Delight

Every dog has his night and tonight is mine!

The Haunting Hound.

At midnight it is time for work. Some places have to be haunted and Mr O'Gool, for one, would never let people down. He and Hairy clock in on the stroke of twelve every night.

Ralph and Mona follow their father for a bit of fiendish fun. They practice uncanny screams and demonic laughs – but still fail to frighten anyone.

"They haven't the knack," says their father, Fingal the Fearsome Phantom. He does not have high hopes for his children.

Shh!!
Silence is essential for a successful haunting.

Mona   Ralph

Daddy

Hairy
x
really
has
disappeared

Hooligans a haunting

Mona and Ralph spend all night trying to distress the neighbors, ringing doorbells, tapping at windows, turning over trashcans. But it has no effect. People have grown used to things that go bump in the night. Nothing surprises them. Even the dogs and cats aren't scared of the two young ghouls. They might just as well have gone to school and learned a bit from their elders.

A Haunting Song
Listen in the dark, listen in the dark
Cats wailing, dogs barking
Trashcans flying, doors banging
Floorboards creaking, taps dripping
Ghosts lurking, ghosts slipping
Silently through the night.

Crying
Cockles
and
mussels

A Night of Toils

With her husband gone a hauntin', Ginny is left at home to play the role of bored houseghost. Light fingered, she tinkles a rag on the grand piano while the vacuum and the broom and the duster dance in appreciation. Housework is a hoot. She is a spook with a sparkle, a specter with splendor.

Meanwhile, Dad is hard at work, nose to the tombstone. In a moment of weakness, he's left his job of haunting the school and is down in the graveyard with a crowd of disreputable, disembodied unearthly beings – his best friends.

Grave Matters

It's tomb opening at the local cemetery.

Nellie Nuisance

Sybil the Sylph

Desmond the Demon

'Good health'

'Cheers'

When Dad rolls home, he kisses his wife (and misses), tells Ralph and Mona they are too bad at haunting to miss a single night at school, tells Float and Gloat they are too young to disappear under his nose and upbraids Hairy and Scary for making themselves so scarce. Then he eats his supper and stands up, the better to tell them a tale or two. And these are the tales he tells.

Baa! Baa!

'Bare' 'Bare'

Boo!

The sheep who spooked
Boo Boo Blacksheep and
made him lose his wool.

The Scarecrow
Spook who could
not scare crows
because he was
invisible.

Ghostly
Ghostly
Gander.

A huge
see-through
goose
who
hurls
people
down the
stairs.

And at the end of the night the O'Gools say their prayers for the living and disappear. They float into a small iron box, bolt its door and wait for night to come again. If you find a locked box in your house do not try to open it.

You never know what will come out.

Good night, sleep tight.

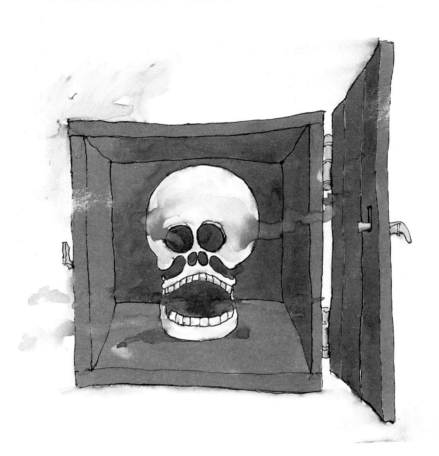

The End